THE
YORK
JOKE BOOK

DALESMAN

Dalesman Publishing Company Ltd
Stable Courtyard, Broughton Hall,
Skipton, North Yorkshire BD23 3AE

First published 1994
Reprinted in this format 1996, 1999, 2001

© Dalesman Publishing Company Ltd

Cover illustration by Silvey Jex
Other cartoons by Crocker

A British Library Cataloguing in Publication record
is available for this book

ISBN 1 85568 081 5

Printed by Amadeus Press, Cleckheaton, West Yorkshire

CONTENTS

5

INTRODUCTION

11

DICTIONARY

*"Are you the chap who phoned about his
brakes?"*

INTRODUCTION

THERE'S nowt so funny as foak, specially wick 'uns.

This proverb typifies the somewhat bawdy humour of the old West Riding - a humour captured by the Victorian dialect writers and transferred to the Music Hall by a succession of Yorkshire comics, one of whom prefaced his act with the words: "Can you hear me, mother?"

Yorkshire folk prefer wit (which is spontaneous) to humour (contrived) and do not like a garrulous person, who might be told: "When t'organ grinder's talking, we can manage ba't monkey."

Yorkshire folk are renowned for their down-to-earthness. Another proverb insists: "Doan't believe all tha sees - fathom it!" And yet another suggests that the Yorkshireman doesn't like wasting time, even when he's dead. He'll "push his way through t'pearly gates, while other folk stand an' staare at 'em."

The Yorkshire type was somewhat intimidating until you got to know it, then you become aware that "a Yorkshireman's heart is like his pudding - crisp outside, but soft within." Now and again, it was important to lay on some charm, for "soft sooap'll greese t'stiffest 'inge."

The women of Yorkshire are indomitable. One who was ceaselessly busy was said to be "as throng as Throp's wife" or, as a moor-edger said, "like an old hen that's got off her eggs and on to t'straw."

Life was always a bit of a lottery. John Thwaite, one of the great dialect writers of the Yorkshire Dales, declared of a lass who could not make up her mind about who to wed - and then picked t'wrong un: "She went through t'wood an' through t'wood an' gat a crewked stick at last." And "some folks are allus leeting on theer feet, while others hezzant a leg ta stand on."

Yorkshire folk like a bit of tom-foolery. Aunt Kate was said to have "allus framed (acted) like a fooil." Aunt Kate is one of the mythical Yorkshire characters. No one remembers a single utterance, but she appears to have been a person who, though basically good-tempered, usually created a muddle of anything she did.

Who was Throp's Wife, who was always throng (busy)? We do not know, but there are many women in Yorkshire who detest idleness and are "as throng as Throp's Wife...shoo wor that throng shoo hanged hersen wi' t'dishclaht."

Another comic character was Tom Pepper, who achieved notoriety as a liar. "He was turned out of hell twice before breakfast for lying." Perhaps Tom was one of those about whom Swift speaks and who improved upon the Devil's invention.

If, in the Yorkshire of many years ago, a child was querulous, mother would say: "You're as queer as Dick's hatband." One small girl thought it was "Dick Satband" until she heard the concluding part of the saying: "...that went nine times round and then wouldn't tie."

"...as mentioned in the advert: this is the half-tiled bathroom..."

Yorkshire humour is noted for its realism but sometimes enters the world of fantasy, as with the story of daft villages like Austwick and Cowling (known to the locals as Cowin'eard). In the Ingleborough Country, the inhabitants of three rival villages had nicknames for each other - Clapham Ducks, Newby Dish-clouts and Austwick Cuckoos. The last-named came in for the lion's share of the abuse.

The story was told of how the wise men of Austwick tried to keep the cuckoo through the winter by building a wall round the tree where she usually roosted. When the cuckoo flew over the wall next morning, one man was convinced that they would have held it if they had built one or two more courses.

Another Austwick tale is of a farm man who was wheeling an empty barrow in and out of a barn. "What's ta laking at?" asked a Clapham man. "T'hay were damp, so I'm just takking a bit o' t'sunshine in to dry it."

Cowling, between Cross Hills and Colne, is noted for its moons. As long ago as 1827, it is recorded (Hone's Table Book) that a local shepherd got as far from home as Skipton (six miles). It was a fine, moonlit night. He remarked to a local man: "Our Cowling moon is just like your Skipton moon."

At Cowling, it was decided, after much controversy, to move the Church tower "a thoathri' yards." A team of well-set-up lads therefore set out to do the job. Having laid their coats on the grass, they walked to the other side of the tower and "gotagate, shovin'." Their coats were stolen.

When they had pushed themselves to a standstill, they walked back round the tower to see how they were progressing and, not seeing their coats, concluded they had pushed the church tower over them. Said the blacksmith, leader of the team: "We'd better push it back."

Almost every village in the old West Riding claims the story of the brass band which got back late at night after winning the band contest. So as not to wake the village, they tip-toed up the main street in their stockinged feet; and at the same time, to mark the triumphant occasion, they played See the Conquering Hero Comes at full blast.

Above all, there's Yorkshire pride. A man in a railway compartment said he could tell where each passenger came from simply by hearing them speak. At length, he turned to a man sitting moping in a corner. "You're the easiest of the lot; you're from Lancashire." The man bestirred himself and said:

"Nay, Ah'm from Yorkshire really. But Ah've bin nobbut badly for three week."

This book of humour is a distillation of 50 years of amusing tales which have appeared in Dalesman. I had the honour to edit the magazine for many years. We allus put folk before things and we found generous space in every issue for stories of the lighter side of Yorkshire life.

The tales are grouped together under subjects which are presented in alphabetical order.

W. R. MITCHELL

DICTIONARY

AGE

A Beverley man who visited an old friend on his 101st birthday shook hands with him and asked him how he was. "Oh, very nicely," said the old man. "Aw'm better on my legs than I was 100 years ago."

A discussion on longevity took place at the Day Centre. An old lady said: "I'd like to see my 100th birthday. If I die at 99 by 'eck - I'll be reet vexed."

ANGLING

An Airedale fisherman, making his way home after a fruitless day's angling, called at a friend's house. "Ah haven't had a bite all t'day," he remarked. The lady of the house jumped to her feet exclaiming: "Eh! What! Ah'll put t'kettle on - thoo'll be fair famished."

ART

A boy in the art class was asked to draw a house. The teacher commented: "What's that funny thing on top?" "A chimney." "But there isn't any smoke." Said the young artist: "They're norrup yet!"

An artist was putting the finishing touches to a

water-colour of a cottage at Robin Hood's Bay when a fisherman glanced over his shoulder, admired the picture and asked what would happen to it. "I may send it to an exhibition - probably in London." The fisherman, much impressed, said: "That's my cottage. Wad you mind paintin' a bit of a noticeboard tellin' folk I let it out in t'summer?"

Percy Monkman was completing a painting in Dent when a shower of rain induced him to take refuge in a large opening next to an inn. A passing resident looked at the picture, then said: "I'll tell thee what, lad. When tha's done it tha wants to take it into t'pub. Thou'll git a fiver for it. I've sin 'em give a fiver for a lot worse na that!"

Two photographers met. One said: "My grannie's just fallen down t'stairs." His friend, much concerned, said: "What did you give her?" He replied: "Oh, a hundredth at f.11."

BEDTIME

When up to t'grandson's little bed
At neet Ah seek to creep,
This thowt is runnin' through me 'ead:
"Ah'll read 'im off to sleep."

An' picking up a book o' rhyme -
Let critics sneer and scoff -
Ah read and read reight up to t'time
At youngster doses off.
But t'oither neet, at t'side o' t'bed -
It 'appens now an' then -
Ah read, an' yawned, an' yawned an' read
An' went to sleep missen.

Grannie suggested to young Catherine that she might count sheep to send her to sleep. Next morning, Catherine said: "I couldn't get to sleep because when I reached 122 I couldn't remember which number came next."

Tha's gor aht t'wrong side o' t'bed.
Tha's argued wi' owt that's bin said.
Even lewked for a feight
Tha should o' gor aht on t'right
But tha gor aht on t'left side instead...

BOOKS

The Eskdale farmer's wife said to her daughter: "I hope that's a nice book you're reading." Her daughter replied: "It's a lovely book, but I don't think you would like it. It's sad at the end. She leaves him and he has to go back to his wife."

CANALS

A bargee was seen cutting two grooves in the masonry of a bridge above the towpath. He said: "My 'oss keeps catchin' 'is lugs on t'bridge." His friend remarked: "Why doesn't tha dig some of t'bank away." "Nay," said the bargee, "it's t'lug's that are catching, not 'is feet."

CHAPEL

On his way to the river Ure one Sunday morning, James Horner was accosted by the vicar. "Nay, Jimmie, not fishing on the Sabbath, surely?" "Aye, it's alright for thee Vicar; thy dinner's in t'oven but mine's still in t'beck."

The new curate mentioned, by mistake, that Christ fed the 5,000 using 2,000 loaves and two small fishes. A Dales farmer was heard to remark: "That's nowt. I could have done it missen." Next Sunday, the curate correctly quoted "two loaves and five small fishes", then leaned over the front of the pulpit and said to the Dales farmer: "I don't think you'd find that so easy now." He replied: "I'd use t'bread left ower frae last Sunda'."

The vicar, when showing the bishop the parish hall, was asked: "What kind of heating is it?" Said the vicar: "Most peculiar."

A teacher asked a small girl what she was drawing. "I'm drawing God," she replied. The teacher said that no one knows what God looks like." The small girl sighed and replied: "They will do when I've finished."

The new vicar asked a farmer if he could find him a nice treble." The farmer looked nervously round and asked: "Which do you want - choir or racing?"

"Daddy," said a Methodist minister's son. "Our teacher says that 'collect' and 'congregate' mean the same thing. Do they?" The minister said: "There's a big difference between a 'collection' and a 'congregation'."

A group of Chapellers called a meeting to discuss the state of the roof. The wealthiest man among them, knowing that he would be expected to fork out much of the estimated £200, insisted that it was not in need of repair. A large piece of plaster detached itself and hit him squarely on the head.

"Well, 'appen it wants mendin'," he conceded, "so I'll give you £100." The minister looked solemnly at the hole in the ceiling and said: "Go on, Lord - hit him again."

A Methodist local preacher went to take a service in a rural chapel at which there was no organ - only a lady pianist. Handing her his list of hymns, he was surprised to be given a list in return. "These are my hymns," she explained. "I can only play on the white notes."

Heard at a chapel in York: "A sermon should last as long as it takes me to suck one or two Polo mints. Tonight, I ate the whole packet."

A West Riding vicar told his congregation that every blade of grass is a sermon.

"See, Soapso Suds keep your hands white and soft."

Next day, as he mowed his lawn, a passing parishioner remarked: "That's reight, vicar, cut thi sermons short!"

Two old dears were talking after the morning service. "When I first married..." began one. "Oh, my dear," interrupted the other. "How many times have you been married?"

A tourist stopped his car and asked directions to the ancient church. A local man pointed to the building, which was in the visible distance, at the end of a long drive. "That's a lengthy drive," observed the tourist. "Aye," said the local, "but if it was any shorter it wouldn't reach t'church."

Two old men stood on Scarborough seafront, admiring the view. One was a staunch atheist and the other a dedicated Methodist. The first man said: "If God's supposed to walk wi' yer all t'time, 'ow cum that when yer walkin' on t'sands there's only one set o' footprints?" Replied the Methodist: "That's because the Lord God's carrying yer on 'is back."

CHILDREN

A busy York man about to dash off to a meeting explained to his small son (who was expecting to have a story read to him) that he was taking the chair at a meeting. The boy remarked: "Have all the others got to stand?"

Six-year-old Sheffield girl to her mother: "If bees make honey, do wasps make marmalade?"

Standing in a shop queue at Beverley was a grubby youngster, aged about five. He sniffed and snuffled. The lady beside him said: "Have you got a hanky?" Glowering, the boy replied: "Aye, but me Mam sez I haven't to lend it to nobody."

A girl who had her first glimpse of the sea at Filey took one look at the most lovely beach in England and shouted - "big baff".

The Pickering lad who climbed on to the wall of an orchard came face to face with the owner, who demanded: "Where are you going?" The lad said, briskly: "Back."

Young Kate was given chocolate to share with her older brother Christopher. Soon afterwards, she ran into the house sobbing and then said: "It's not fair. I broke it exactly in half and he took the biggest half!"

A Dales lad visited his aunt in Selby. As she summoned him to the table prior to the start of the meal, he eyed his side plate with misgivings. "Surely you have plates at home," said his aunt. "Aye," replied the lad, "but not wi' nowt on 'em."

Harry did not want to have his face washed. Grandma explained that she had washed her face three times a day ever since she was a little girl. Harry looked at her face and said: "And look how it's shrunk!"

Said Betty to her mother: "Don't wash my face today; it's got a smile on."

"Ma, Tom wants half the bed." "That's all right, dear." "Mum - he wants his half in the middle."

CLOTHING

He stroked his suit; he felt reight chuffed;
He knew they'd not a clue.
It wasn't suit he'd 'ad for years -
But t'other half of two.

COURTING

A timid young man and his girl stood watching two cows rubbing their faces together. "Tha knaws, lass, I could do that," he said. She replied: "Ah can't stop tha. It's not my cow."

A courting couple walked across the fields. He

said: "What's ta bin thinkin', lass." "Nowt much," she whispered. "What? Doan't you think about me?" "I was."

CRAFTSMEN

The blacksmith told a customer a small welding job would cost "six bob". The customer, having converted this to new pence, said: "Haven't you changed to decimal currency yet?" The blacksmith replied: "Nay - I doan't think it'll tak on."

The visitor from London who watched a traditional Yorkshire Dales blacksmith making a wrought-iron gate said it was wonderful to see a true craftsman at work. "I am employed in the small instrument field, where we've got to be accurate to 1/10,000th of an inch." The blacksmith said, quietly: "Ah's exact."

CYCLING

Two cyclists left Halifax for a Whitsuntide run in 1920. A pall of smoke hung over West Riding towns most days of the year. One cyclist said: "What's that funny smell?" The other replied: "I think it must be fresh air."

A short-sighted cyclist at York,
Was teaching his parrot to talk;
When perched on his neck
It gave him a peck;
The cyclist fell off with a squawk!

DEATH

A junior reporter in Batley called at a house in the town to get particulars about a man who had died. The widow was friendly and asked if he would like to see the body. Unable to refuse, he did so and, feeling some comment was called for, expressed the view that he looked very peaceful. She looked at the corpse closely and said: "Aye, he does an' all, doesn't he? But he always were a bit slow on the uptake, were Albert, so happen he hasn't tumbled to what's happened to him yet."

DENTISTRY

The Daleswoman, who was busy cleaning up in the house, was not wearing her new set of dentures. When a friend asked if they hurt her, she replied: "Nay, but I'm not paying a lot o' brass for teeth to cleean up in."

DOCTORS

When the village gossip was asked about Lizzie, she replied: "Lizzie's looking more like now t'doctors have finished wi' her. You can tell how bad she was. When they oppened 'er up, t'moths flew out."

Doctor to patient, who is in his 70s: "Well now, you've had your three score years and ten, you know." The patient replied: "Nay, doctor - tha hasn't allowed for V.A.T."

A doctor who rebuked a dalesman for walking about for several days with a broken arm said he should have been consulted. The dalesman replied: "Every time Ah says something is wrang wi' me, t'wife maks me stop smoking."

An Austwick man caught by heavy rain while visiting the doctor in Settle was loaned an umbrella by the doctor, who unfurled it before handing it over. The patient, who had never seen an umbrella before, reached home but could not get the umbrella into the house. He attached it to a piece of clothes-line and hauled it up to a bedroom window, but it was too large for the hole. "Eh, we mun tether it to t'post in t'paddock until next Tuesday." The following Tuesday, the Austwick man combined business with his visit to the doctor and marched triumphantly back to Settle with the umbrella outspread. It was a sunny, cloudless day!

DO-IT-YOURSELF

A neighbour found a man scraping wallpaper off the walls. Was he re-decorating? "Nay," was the reply. "We're moving house."

Extracted from a police accident report: "I looked for the sign but the more I looked the more I couldn't find it."

ENTERTAINMENT

The television set at a Wharfedale farm was decrepit. Asked if he was thinking of buying another television, the farmer remarked: "I've nobbut getten used to t'fowk on this set."

FARMING

A farmer was driving sheep on the moor just below Cowling Crag when a woman rushed out of a moor-edge house and told him to remove the sheep; the moor belonged to her. Six months later, he saw furniture and other possession stacked outside the woman's house. "Ar'ta flittin'?" he asked her. "Aye, we're going to Bradla'." The farmer, recalling her claim she owned the moor, said: "I wish I'd known. I'd have given you a hand wi' t'Pinnacle."

A shepherd entered Tan Hill inn. Seated in the room was a young mother with a baby of tender age. Casting a glance in the direction of the child, the shepherd remarked: "Ay, lad, I wish I was as awd as thee." Then, doubtless thinking he might be mistaken about the child's sex, he asked the mother: "I'st a tup or a gimmer?"

"My dog's that intelligent if it saw t'hoose burning - it'd dart in and come out wi' t'insurance policy."

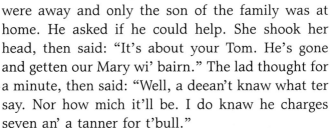

A notice "Beware of the Bull" stood at the edge of a field. On the nearby gate was a second notice: "Survivors please close this gate."

An agitated farmer's wife visited the next farm, but discovered that the parents were away and only the son of the family was at home. He asked if he could help. She shook her head, then said: "It's about your Tom. He's gone and getten our Mary wi' bairn." The lad thought for a minute, then said: "Well, a deean't knaw what ter say. Nor how mich it'll be. I do knaw he charges seven an' a tanner for t'bull."

A farmer knocked at the pearly gate,
His face was scarred and old;
He stood before the man of fate,
For admission to the Fold.
"What have you done," St Peter asked,
"To gain admission here?"
"I've been a farmer, sir," he said,
"For many and many a year."
The pearly gate swung open wide,
As St Peter touched the bell.
"Come in," he said, "and choose your harp...
"You've had your taste of hell."

Jimmy was annoying his dad, a busy farmer, by asking endless questions. What makes lightning? What causes an earthquake? "Eeh, I only wish I could tell thee," replied Dad on each occasion. Jimmy asked if he was being a nuisance, asking all the questions. "Nay, lad," said his father, "tha'll nivver learn nowt unless tha asks."

A farmer at Clayton West asked his son to fetch one of the two horses from the field and harness it to the trap to take him to Barnsley. "Which horse shall I fetch, dad?" "Bring t'oldest - we'll use t'oldest up first." The lad remarked: "In that case, dad, I think thou'd better go for it."

The farmhand arrived at the village stores with a yard brush in two pieces. "Can you sell me a new sweeping brush, please?" he asked. "T'handles come out o' this 'un four times this morning, and now t'blooming head's gone and fell off."

The Wetherby farmer was deeply engrossed in reading The Farmer and Stockbreeder. His wife repeatedly asked him a question but received no reply. In exasperation, she snatched the magazine out of his hand and said: "Why don't you answer when I'm speaking to you." He replied: "How can ah hear when ah'm not listening?"

A Todmorden farmer met a Land Girl who had both hands stuffed in her breeches pockets. She said: "I say, mister, is this the way to Oldham?" The farmer replied: "I doan't rightly knaw. I wear braces on mine."

Two Dales farmers were in friendly competition. Each had a goat. "My goat can beat thine - he can jump o'er two barrels laid side by side," said one. "That's nowt. Mine can sing. Yours can't." "Well, no - but she 'hums' a bit now and again."

A Moors man went to York, where he met an old school friend. They had a few drinks and ate supper at the friend's house. It was too late for the

Moors man to return home, so he stayed the night. Next morning, his friend asked him if he had slept well, adding: "I heard a noise like a car; I hope it did not disturb you." Said the Moors man: "That was me. Your pyjamas didn't quite fit me, so I went home for mine."

When farmers made butter, which they sold to local grocers, one of the grocers had a feeling he was getting short weight. He asked the farmer how he went about weighing the butter. Said the farmer: "I weighs it against thy sugar."

A visitor, amused by local farming terms, asked a farmer what was the different between "muck" and "clarts", to be told: "Muck's muck dry an' clarts is muck wet."

An accountant who was helping an old farmer to sort out his affairs said: "Will your records be kept on a computer?" The farmer said: "My records'll be kept on t'same bloody spike they've allus bin kept on!"

Old Mary never beat about the bush. Dissatisfied with the quality of the milk she collected each morning from a neighbouring farm, she took two jugs instead of one and remarked: "Ah' have milk i' one and watter in t'other - and I'll mix me own!"

It was a wet haytime. The farmer looked gloomily around the table, where three or four of his monthly haytime men were having a meal. He was heard to say:

T'wind blaes, t'wrack rides,

Meeat gangs, t'hay bides.

The undertaker, having measured up the dear-departed for his coffin, said to the widow: "When shall we bury 'im? How aboot next Friday?" She replied: "That'll be aw reet." Another long silence, then the eldest son remarked: "No, that wean't do." "Why not?" "T'bull sale at 'Awes."

When television came to the dale, a boastful farmer said: "I've got ITV." His friend remarked: "Mine's just as 'igh as thine."

An old and somewhat short-tempered Wolds farmer had a dog which was not shaping well. In desperation and truly vexed, he shouted: "Thoo useless b... Coom 'ere an' 'old this gate oppen while I drive 'em through messen."

A Yorkshire farmer travelled by rail with his young son, who was a big lad. The farmer bought a whole ticket for himself and a half ticket for his son. The ticket collector accepted the farmer's ticket but claimed the son was too old to qualify for half fare.

Said the farmer: "That's thy fault. He were nobbut a lad when he left York."

A city motorist stopped on Blakey Ridge and asked a farmer the way to Rosedale Abbey. "There's a signpost half a mile down the road." The motorist, in a teasing mood, said he couldn't read. The farmer replied: "Well, that sign'll suit thee - there's nowt on it."

A townswoman who asked a farmer if her dog (a Corgi) would be suitable for working on the land was told: "It'll 'appen be awreight wi' a flock o' hamsters."

"By gum, lad, but last neet's gale did a lot o' damage on my farm. Did it harm yours?" "I doan't rightly know." "Nay - thou must know if owt's damaged." "Well I don't. It's barn roof. I haven't found it yet."

Local builders had to visit a remote farm. One of their number was sent to a farm to hire a horse. The farmer wanted to assess how much to charge, so he asked: "How long will you want it?" The man replied: "As long as you've got; there's three of us."

FAMILIES

Two old men were discussing the size of families. One said: "I'd eleven, all lasses. I'd a' liked a cricket team. I git a sewing class."

Prof. James Wright, a distinguished scholar and Professor of Philosophy at the University of Oxford early this century, was a Yorkshireman from a humble home. One day, he was showing his elderly mother round the Oxford colleges. When they reached All Souls, she commented: "Eh, it would make a grand Co-op."

FOOD

A schoolboy, asked about salt, replied: "It's the stuff that makes potatoes taste nasty when Mum forgets to put it in."

A parson, visiting a Wensleydale cottage, listened delightedly as the housewife sang: "Nearer, my God, to thee." She explained: "It's the hymn I boil eggs to - one verse for soft and two for hard."

Some folk like faggots and some like cow
'eel, While others is partial to chips;
And some Yorkshire folk love their
savoury duck, While tripe nivver passes
their lips...

Young George whispered to his mother: What's my
uncle dewin' usin' 'is knife ter eyt 'is peas?" "Eh,
lad," chortled mother, "tha dun't need fret abaht
yon, for 'e's brass enough to use a shovel if he's
minded."

A conjuror was appearing at a village hall in
Wharfedale. A thrifty man bought his wife a ticket
for the show and said that when the conjuror came
to that part where he took a teaspoonful of flour
and one egg and made 20 omelettes, she must
"watch verra, verra close."

Two Leeds businessmen took advantage of the
lunch hour to visit Headingley Cricket Ground to
watch a particularly interesting match. One of them
called out to a boy, gave him a shilling and said:
"Bring three fourpenny meat pies from the corner
shop. If you're quick, you can have a pie for
yourself." The lad returned, breathless but
triumphant. "Eightpence change," he gasped.
"They nobbut had my pie left."

"What kind o' meat is that? asked the city shopper. "It's a pig's head," the butcher informed her. "I know that," the visitor replied immediately. "What I meant was, is it beef or is it mutton?"

A Keighley man entered a fishmonger's shop and commented on the dearness of the crabs. "Ah can gerrem at arf that price at t'other shop." The fishmonger wondered why he did not buy the crabs there. Said the customer: "Cos they eh none."

A man well-known for his enormous appetite would eat a gluttonous lunch, then sit back in his chair, light his pipe and say: "Well, na' then, we'll etta 'pine' woll teatime."

The father of a large family was getting flustered, while carving a roast rabbit, when each of his children demanded a leg. He eventually said: "I'se carving a rabbit - not a centipede."

Overheard in a fish and chip shop: "Fish and chips, twice." The shop owner replied: "Alright; I heard you the first time."

Two men from South Yorkshire were looking over the harbour wall after strolling out of the pub. "Why, thus noa watter in here, Tom." Said Tom: "I'm not surprised; they'll sup owt here."

The toper awoke in the late morning with "a shocking head". He told a friend: "If I'd known I felt so bad, I wouldn't have woken up so early."

A Yorkshireman sitting in the hotel lounge while on holiday in Paris turned to the man on his left with the greeting: "Bonsoir, Monsieur." He received the reply: "Ich Deutsche." He tried the same greeting with the man on his right, who turned out to be Spanish. Approaching the only customer at the bar, he asked: "Parleyvous, Francais?" "Aye, lad," was the immediate and unexpected reply, "tha comes fraw Yorksher an' all. What'll ta 'ave to drink?"

GARDENING

On market day at Otley a market gardener who had medicinal herbs as an extra told a farmer: "There's nowt in t'pain line but there's an herb to shift it." Unimpressed, the farmer said: "What's ta getten for heartache." The market gardener replied: "If tha's smittled wi' that, there's nowt for it but - thyme."

An elderly Dalesman, visiting a garden centre, was shown a sundial and given an explanation as to how it worked. He remarked: "Whatever will they think of next?"

A market gardener, taking his young son to Leeds for the first time, rapped hard on the pavement with his stick and then looked meaningly at his son. "Now tha knaws why they've got towns - t'ground's too hard to rotovate."

A young student sought to impress an old market gardener by telling him that all his methods were wrong. The old man thought little of the argument and smiled contemptuously, upon which the young man said: "Well, I think I ought to know. I've studied at two different agricultural colleges."

The old man remarked: "I once worked on a farm where we

"Does giving up smoking make you feel irritable, Fred?"

had a cawf 'at sucked two different cows." "What's that to do with it?" "Nay, nowt, 'cept more it sucked t'bigger yon cawf grew."

HOLIDAYS

An old man from Hawes paid his first visit to London and stood outside the Mansion House watching traffic. A policeman remarked: "Busy, isn't it?" "Aye," said the old man, "there's a trip in frae Hawes."

A boy told an elderly neighbour he had been on holiday at Blackpool. "Did you go on a donkey?" asked the neighbour. The lad replied: "No - I went by bus."

LAW

The farmer who outlined a case to a solicitor was told: "That chap hasn't a leg to stand on. I'll start at once. In law, the thing's as plain as..." Said the farmer: "Hod on, lad. I don't think we'll tak it any further. I'se just given thee t'other chap's side of t'argument."

A sad little man wandered along the corridors of a suite of offices used by the Inland Revenue. A member of the staff asked if she could help. "Nay, lass," he said. "I just thought I'd take a look at t'folk the law says I've got to work for."

LITERATURE

In an apocryphal story of J.B. Priestley, as related by H.L. Gee, a gushing admirer exclaims: "Oh, Mr Priestley, I think your Angel Pavement the most wonderful book ever written!" Scowling, Priestley is reported to have snapped: "And what's wrong with The Good Companions?"

LOVE

An amorous boatman of Staithes
Catches fishes whenever he bathes,
The fish fills his larder
The sea cools his ardour
Oh, pity the females of Staithes.

H.L. Gee tells the story of an elderly Flamborough woman who, when asked what her husband did, shrugged her shoulders and said: "Oh, he nobbut sits aboot tellin' folks what weather's gannin' ti be termorrer." "He something of a prophet, then?" "Not he - he's nobbut a dead loss."

Gee also related that a couple sitting in the Italian Gardens at Scarborough, on a summer evening, found themselves looking down on a romantic young couple who were talking in hushed tones. The wife whispered: "I think he's going to propose; give a cough or something to warn him." Her husband said: "Why should I? Nobody warned me."

MANHOOD

A son rose from his bed on his 21st birthday and shouted to his dad to tell him there was now a man in the house. "Chuck 'im out, then," said dad. "Just thee try," challenged the lad.

The farmer's wife received a call from a somewhat distressed neighbour who informed her that her son had been "carrying on" with her daughter and that the lass was expecting a baby. What was she going to do about it? At this juncture, the farmer returned for his dinner. His sole comment, when informed of his son's misdeeds, was: "Eeh, the young devil, eel be smokin' next."

"Where's the master of this house?" inquired a salesman. The boy who answered the door said: "She's in t'kitchen."

MEDICINE

A Dales farmer had effective treatment for rheumatism. He complained that "now I can't tell when its bahn ta rain."

"Are you under t'doctor yet?" "Aye". "What sort o' tablets is ta taking?" "White uns. What's thine like?" "They're white uns." "What do they call 'em?" "As before." "Mine isn't same; they're called 'As directed'."

An Airedale plumber was roused at night by the local doctor, who reported that there was a blockage in his toilet. The plumber protested about the lateness of the hour, but the doctor was adamant that something should be done about it immediately. The plumber arrived at the doctor's house, and with the doctor looked at the blocked toilet. Then the plumber remarked: "I'll tell thee what: I'll drop an Aspro down yon toilet, and if it's no better in t'morning, give me another ring."

MILLDOM

Fred was habitually late in turning up for work at a Dewsbury mill in the old days, when bosses were present early in the morning to check the men and women through the gate. One morning, the boss said, gruffly, to Fred: "Doesn't tha knaw t'buzzer's gone?" Fred shook his head sadly and replied: "They'll tak owt these days."

A newly-appointed (and therefore unknown) factory inspector visited a Yorkshire mill. He stopped a man in a cloth cap and announced: "I am His Majesty's Inspector of Factories." The man looked at him, then said solemnly - "And does 'Is Majesty knaw yer 'ere?"

Two married women worked next to each other in a woollen mill in Dewsbury; they were weary of their jobs and wanted to leave. One succeeded, and told her friend she had simply mentioned to her husband that the foreman was making eyes at her. "My hubby said I'd to leave straight away." The second woman decided to do likewise. She told her husband that the foreman kept winking at her. "Ee! That's a good sign," he said. "Wink back at him a few times and mebbe you'll get another couple o' looms."

"How's business?" "Terrible - even them at don't intend to pay aren't buying owt."

A man retiring after 50 years service was presented with a clock by the company's managing director, who shook hands and said: "Least said the best. Tek it and be off."

MONEY

A miserly farmer, when told that a nephew, his sole legatee, would soon squander his inheritance, replied: "Well, if lad gets half as much pleasure spending it as I had making it - he'll do varra weel."

A joiner went to a Yorkshire woodyard and asked for some 3in x 2in posts. The yardman said that everything was now metric. The size required was 7.5 cm x 5 cm. The joiner was surprised and bewildered. He asked how much the material would cost. The yardman said: "Two bob a foot."

An insurance agent approached a retired villager, hoping to interest him in fire insurance for a new cottage. Nay - there's no fires to insure, lad," was the reply. "We've had t'fireplaces bricked up."

Two old ladies were looking into the window of a posh china shop in Leeds. One said: "Just look at t'price o' that plate." The other replied: "Oh, yes, lass - but that's proper pot."

A Yorkshireman went to London and opened a fish and chip shop. A friend, noticing how he had prospered, said: "I reckon if thou lent me two hundred quid, I could open a shop in 'Uddersfield and I'd soon be able to pay you back." The

Yorkshireman replied: "Sorry, lad, but since I came here I've had an understanding wi' t'Bank of England. If I don't lend brass, they won't sell fish and chips."

"Can ta lend me a bob, George?" "Sorry, lad - I've nobbut a shilling as Ah lend out, but if tha can get it back, tha can borrow it." "Who has it?" "Thou 'as."

A Wakefield man said to a friend: "I'm sorry your missus is still in hospital. It must be costing you a pretty penny." "Nay," was the reply, "it's all on t'National Health - and while she's in there she's spending nowt."

On the sea front at Redcar, two boys filled themselves with ice-cream, peanuts and lollipops. An old lady who was sitting on a public seat nearby said: "You must have cost your mother a mint o' money." One lad replied: "Nay - she gorrus on t'National Health."

A Yorkshireman was travelling by train when he heard a Scot bragging about his country. The exasperated Yorkshireman remarked: "Tha's bin opening thi mouth wide about what tha can do. Now tell mi summat tha can't do - and Ah'll do it for thi." Said the Scotsman: "Weel - Ah canna pay ma fare."

Ben, the Askrigg blacksmith, undertook to put a defective pump in order. When it was working again, and money had exchanged hands, someone asked him what he used to clean it out. Was there some special tool? "Nay," replied Ben, "nobbut superior knowledge."

MUSIC

Heard after a male voice choir rehearsal: "I'se fed up wi' all this new-fangled stuff. Why can't we learn summat we know?"

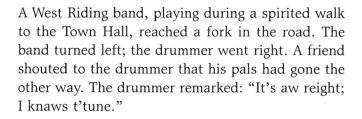

A bluff West Riding councillor introduced the touring Halle Orchestra, under Sir John Barbirolli, as "Mr Barry Brolly and his band."

A West Riding band, playing during a spirited walk to the Town Hall, reached a fork in the road. The band turned left; the drummer went right. A friend shouted to the drummer that his pals had gone the other way. The drummer remarked: "It's aw reight; I knaws t'tune."

NOTICES

Outside a cobbler's shop: "The Devil wants your souls to ruin; I want them to mend."

At a Yorkshire Chapel: "The coming of the Lord draweth nigh. Entrance at the side door."

OLD AGE

When Bert retired from the pithead, he spent all his time at the club or watching television at home. His wife did not think much of this way of life. She said: "I'm not going to get old that way." Bert said: "Nay, lass, tha wor young wi' ma; tha' mun be old wi' ma."

An old lady lost the sight in one eye. When she next visited the optician, she said: "Think on, then, nobbut charge half-price."

OFF-COMERS

Overheard at Grassington Police Station: "And your wife lost her bracelet on the stepping stones across the Wharfe?" "Yes." "How can you be sure?" "That's where she fell in."

"All these new folks," groaned a native-born in the Dales. Then, with the usual twinkle in his blue eyes, he added: "They'll tek some training."

A new-settler in the Dales said to a farmer: "I expect you have to live for 100 years in this place before you're accepted." "Nay, lass, it's nivver as long as that. And if tha's got a greet granddad ligging in t'churchyard, thou's yan of us."

A Yorkshireman did not care for the soft southern approach to retailing. The salesman said: "Sir, what is your pleasure?" Replied the Yorkshireman: "Whippets and rugby league football, if it's owt to do wi' thee. But just nah, I'd like a new suit."

PETS

A lady who kept a budgie thought it looked lonely and decided to buy it a mate. This she did, but on looking into the cafe the next morning she found the new bird was dead. The old budgie looked very sprightly. The lady borrowed an owl from the zoo and put that in the cage. Next morning, the owl was dead and the budgie was looking very cheeky. So the lady borrowed an eagle from the zoo and put it in the cage. Next morning, the eagle was lying dead. The budgie being featherless, its owner asked whatever it had done to itself. The budgie replied: "Oh, I'm alright but I 'ad to take mi jacket off to that 'un."

POACHER

An old poacher was lying seriously ill. One day, he was visited by his arch enemy, the game keeper. Almost at his last gasp, the poacher consented to be reconciled to the gamekeeper and a touching scene followed in which both men shook hands in mutual forgiveness. At the door, the gamekeeper was called back. The old poacher, raising himself in bed, gasped: "But thou mun remember, Fred, if Ah should 'appen to get better - all this is off!"

PROVERBS

Never go to t'auction with a nodding acquaintance.

T'chap 'at gits up wi' t'lark hasn't had one t'evening afore.

RAILWAYS

The knack of using the injectors of City of Wells was being discussed over a pint. "You've got to surprise it - like you would a lavatory cistern." Said another railway fan: "Well, it is a W.C. Class."

A railwayman travelling to York
Got to Selby and took the wrong fork.
Tore his tickets asunder
And threw 'em in t'Humber
And reckoned that next time
he'd walk.

RAMBLING

"You should never have picked Morecambe Bay, mate."

A party of ramblers, knowing nothing of the district, were looking over the amazing collection of Norber boulders above Crummack-dale, close to the village of Austwick. A knowing local lad spoke about the Ice Age and said the rocks had been brought to their present position by a glacier. "What happened to the glacier?" asked one of the ramblers. The local lad thought for a moment, then said: "'Appen it went back for some more rocks."

'Twas autumn at a Yorkshire inn,
The rain poured down without.
He entered soaking to the skin -
A hiker and a waterspout.
He'd trodden o'er the sodden moor,
He oozed from boot to tie,
And as the streams flowed on the floor
"A drink!" he cried, "I'm dry."

After a lengthy walk and with a hearty appetite, a rambler reached a village cafe which had a sign announcing: "Beans, Spam and Chips". He went inside and asked if there was anything else on the menu. "Of course," said the proprietor, who then listed: Bacon, Spam and Chips; Mushy Peas, Spam and Chips; Sausage, Spam and Chips and - Spam and Chips.

Two Victorian ramblers always put their best feet forward when they saw a church steeple because "it's ten-to-one there'll be a pub next to it."

SCHOOL

Young Fred returned from school on his first day and was asked by grannie what he had been doing. He said: "All sorts - painting, crayoning, singing.

But I'm not going back tomorrow." "Why?" Young Fred sighed before remarking: "You can't shift for flippin' kids."

A Pakistani boy started school in a West Yorkshire town. One of the class, reporting on this to his mother, was asked: "Do you know where Pakistan is?" The lad didn't know, but added: "It can't be so far - he goes home for his dinner."

A farmer's lad arrived home from school with news that he had put down his name for a trip. Grandfather handed him a £10 note, adding: "If you don't spend it, let me have it back." The trip took place, the farmer's son returned, Grandfather asked him if he had any money left, and was told: "Yes - but I spent your £10 first."

The school register was full. The classroom was packed. The teacher said to a lad who came to see him: "It's very generous of you, young Jack, but I don't think your resignation would be much help in this situation."

A teacher who was taking a class on a nature walk asked a farmer's son how many sheep he could count in a nearby pasture. He replied, with an air of pitying superiority: "Them's noan sheep. Them's bluddy tups."

The boy who returned home from his school outing to Haworth, in the Bronte Country, said he had seen the Worth Valley Railway, the Bronte Waterfall, Bronte Parsonage and Bronte teashops. He'd also been to Haworth Zoo he added, mischievously, and had seen a - Bronteasurus.

The schoolteacher who was instructing the class on the various months of the year came to March and asked: "What comes in like a lion and goes out like a lamb?" A boy replied: "Me dad."

"Look at that old tree. If that ash tree could speak, what would it say to me?" a teacher said to a farmer's son during a school nature walk. He said: "It'd say - I'm an oak tree, miss."

SEASIDE

Overheard at Bridlington was this conversation between a child and harassed mum: "Ah want to go on t'sands!" "Well, yer can't." "Well, why can't Ah?" "Cos t' tide's in." "But why can't Ah go on t'sands?" "Cos there's watter all ower 'em. Theer!"

A Northallerton man who was visiting a Yorkshire coast resort patronised a fortune teller who said he would be very poor until he reached middle age.

The visitor asked what would happen later. The fortune teller said: "After that time, you'd have got used to it."

SHIPPING

Overheard in the office of a shipping agent, following a radio talk with a ship in the Humber: "How the hell can he go 'full ahead' with the anchor still down?"

SHOPPING

A shopper at a stall in Hawes market noticed two girls who had been gazing at a stall advertising Moleskin Trousers. One girl remarked: "They must breed some big moles round here. Look at those trousers. You can't even see the join!"

A village butcher was such a friendly soul he found it difficult to stop talking to a customer. A busy lady poked her head around the shop door and shouted: "A pund o' steak, Jimmy, an' ah'll call for t'pedigree in' t'morning."

A boy asked for a tablet of toilet soap. The shopkeeper said: "Do you want it scented?" "No, thanks - I can carry it home missen."

SPEECH

Members of a West Yorkshire men's club were giving a dinner in honour of a famous man. The mayor, who presided, spoke at such tedious length that the man on his left picked up the gavel and took a swipe at his head. He missed the chairman but hit the guest of honour, who slumped down in his seat murmuring: "Hit me again! I can still hear him!"

Tha' can say what tha' likes to a Yorkshireman;
Tha' can do as tha' likes an' all;
But tha'll gerrit all back an' more besides
So mind wot tha' sez, that's all!

A Dales farmer asked the telephone operator for "one-nuthin-nought-nowt". The operator was quick on the uptake and put him through to 1000.

A Cleckheaton woman told the operator: "I've given you a lot of trouble so I'm putting an extra coin in the slot for yourself."

The Yorkshirewoman who was being interviewed for a job in London spoke so broadly the prospective employer said: "Don't you know the Queen's English?" She said: "Aye, lad - they wouldn't have a foreigner on t'throne."

A Bradfordian was describing a visit to London to someone who had not been there before. "Well, owd lad, tha's bin to Leeds, an't tha? Weel, it's like that - only wuss."

Shoo's as thin as a lahtle bit of soap after a lang day's washing.

(Of a fat man). There goes Jack o' Bills carryin' all afore 'im.

Some men'll mak hay wi t'grass as grows under uther chaps' feet.

A gooid way to stop a chap's maath is to keep yer awn shut.

A chap 'at's liberal wi' advice is generally niggardly wi' brass.

Overheard on the telephone: "Hello, is that thee? Aye, this is me. Tha nawse that theer I were tellin' thee abaat? Well, I've gitten it. I'll see thee toneet."

"Oh, aye, t'owd vicar's finished bud he weean't stop."

A Yorkshire banquet - bread and cheese and a chap you can talk to.

A Cockney was continually teasing a Yorkshireman about his accent. The final straw came when the Cockney said: "They're all a bit fick up North, ain't they?" The Yorkshireman said: "I've always been told t'densest population were in London."

SPORT

A visitor to a remote railway station saw it was deserted except for the stationmaster and porter. They were playing cricket. Try as he would, the porter could not take the wicket of the stationmaster. The visitor picked up the ball and the innings ended abruptly. Grasping him warmly by the hand, the porter said: "Eh, lad, I'm glad you did that. He's bin in for four years."

When the name of a one-time famous member of a Yorkshire Rugby Club appeared in the New Year's Honour's List under those who were knighted, he received a telegram from former members of the club which read: "If t'Queen knew thee like we know thee, she wouldn't tap thee on t'shoulder wi' her sword; she'd chop thi head off."

The groundsman at a Five-a-Side charity match commented: "It were a poor turn out awtogether. There were a lot o' folk theer as nivver turned up."

At a Sunday cricket league match at Scarborough, Yorkshire were being trounced by Middlesex. A programme seller met with only moderate sales until the ground was invaded by greenfly. He quickly changed his cry from "Programmes and score-cards, 20p" to "Greenfly swatters, 20p" and soon sold out.

Jackie, the opening bat, was in tremendous form when playing for the village team in Harewood Park. When the bowler sent him a short one down, on the leg side, Jackie went down on one knee and hooked it with tremendous power. The

"That's the mole flap."

ball soared over the boundary. Suddenly, the church clock - a quarter of a mile away - struck the hour. One of the supporters remarked: "By lad, what a heave; he's hitten t'clock."

Old Tom's eyesight was so bad, he could not get a place in the first team for cricket. One weekend, when the team was short of players, a friend suggested he might lodge a cricket ball in the guttering of the pavilion and lure his skipper on to the wicket. He could then draw the skipper's attention to the ball. He was sure to get a place in the premier team on the following Saturday. This did not happen. As he explained to a friend: "On t'way back to t'pavilion, I fell over t'roller."

George, who was one of the men who keepered the grouse moors around Simon's Seat in Wharfedale in the days when George V never missed the Twelfth, had a gun accident which necessitated amputation of his right leg. Returning to his cottage to convalesce, the primitive sanitation called for the use of a bedpan and, mastering this, considering his bulk and the loss of a leg, was no easy matter. For the first time, he sat there, uttering belly-rumbling chuckles. His wife asked him what he was laughing at. George replied: "Now I know what t'owd hen feels like when she's sittin' a pot egg."

The hunter crouches in his blind
Neath camouflage of every kind
And conjures up a quacking noise
To lend allure to his decoys;
This grown-up man with pluck and luck
Is hoping to outwit...a duck.

An argument had arisen during a game of snooker as to whether two balls were touching. An old chap in the corner said: "Tha' can see from 'ere, white 'uns touchin' but t'red 'un in't."

TIME

There's nivver nowt but what there's summat,
And when there's summat it's offen nowt;
And them that allus think they're summat
Has nearly allus risen fra nowt.
It's no use sitting an' waiting for summat,
Cos more often it nobbut ends wi' nowt -
And come to think on't, these lines I've penned
Are maistly summat abaht nowt.

TRAVEL

A lorry driver was enjoying a meal in a cafe beside the Great North Road in North Yorkshire. Three motor cyclists swaggered in, spoiling for a fight. The driver was just about to tackle his steak pie and chips when one of the leather-jacket gang took his meal, another tipped his fruit salad on to the floor and the third drank his coffee. The lorry driver did nothing about it. He paid his bill and walked out. One of the trouble-makers approached the waitress and commented: "He wasn't much of a man." She replied: "He's not much of a driver either; he's just run over three motor bikes."

In the Grosmont-Egton district, a lady stopped her car on a steep hill to ask a local woman, who stood at her garden gate: "Is this hill dangerous?" The reply was: "Not up here - it's down at t'bottom where they all kills thersens."

Bert was off to Kuwait to work. Someone asked his aunt which way he would go. "Nay, I've no idea - but he's got to change at Harrogate."

A visitor to the village commented to an elderly resident: "I understand this is an ancient Roman road." "Nay," was the reply, "I've lived here all mi life, but I've nivver sin any Romans come along 'ere - 'cept for a few Iti's during t'last war."

When people from Devon see Robin Hood's Bay,
In actual fact, or on telly,
I blow off my top if, in passing, they say:
"Ah, wonderful! Yorkshire's Clovelly!"
But if I should get to Clovelly one day,
I'll murmur: "My word! Why, it's heaven",
And ere any native can offer his say:
"The Robin Hood's Bay of Old Devon."

A woman in a station refreshment room was struggling with a cup of coffee as her train came in. She endeavoured to gulp it quickly. A dalesman sitting at the next table noticed her plight. He leaned across to her and said: "Here, mum, you tak' my cup o' coffee. Ah've already saucered and blowed it."

Grannie drew the head of Skipton High Street for her four-year-old grandson and he was quite impressed until a small figure was added. "Who is that?" "It's you." "Can't be - I'm not allowed to go out on my own."

An off-comed-un who arrived at Silsden asked the way to Willie Inman's house and was told: "Go up theer, an' turn ower John Berry brig, an' then goa past Joan o' Wills, past Sammy Shoemaker's, on bi Tom o' Bills, through t'Bell Square, past owd Dick Wood's, ower t'street brig, then turn up at Cat Hoil end, goa past Henry o' Joss's an' tha' almost theer - he lives anant Nan o' Simons."

"There are some nosey people around here."

A Portuguese guide was extolling the bridge across the Tagus as the longest suspension bridge in Europe. "Oh no it isn't," chorused the Yorkshire tourists, "our Humber Bridge is the longest." The guide said: "The Japanese are starting what will be the longest suspension bridge in the world." Said the Tykes: "It still won't be as long as ours."

TROUBLE

At Castleton, in Eskdale, young horse riders were displaying their prowess over the jumps. As one approached an awkward jump, his horse seemed to hesitate. Loud and clear over the loudspeaker system came the remark: "Come on, John - never let it be said thee mother bred a jibber."

A man was taken to the top of a Yorkshire dale; he looked around him, and said: "I reckon this is where God brok 'is shovel."

The veteran farmer was worried about sex. "Surely not at your age," said a friend in whom he confided. "Aye, lad - we've had a record crop o' taties and I haven't enough sex to put 'em in."

"Why meet trouble hawf way, I says. If thou waits long enuff, it'll come to thee."

H.L. Gee told about a farmer who saw a farm man one morning and commented he never expected to meet him so far from home. The labourer said: "Ah've left mi job...A while sin an owd coo died, and for weeks we'd nowt to eat on t'farm but beef. Then an owd sheep died, and we'd nowt but mutton. Noo, t'owd woman's died - and so Ah've left."

Gee also related that Joe Murgatroyd, the West Riding "great daft chump", was seen early one morning as he tried to poke bits of stick under his front door. Someone asked him what was wrong. "Ivverything," growled Joe. "Ah'm in a reet mess. T'wife's i' bed and shoo told ma to put t'key through t'letterbox when I went to t'mill. Well, Ah've done as shoo said but, dang it, Ah forgot to lock t'door furst. Now Ah can't reach t'key nohow."

WEATHER

In the early days of radio, a Leeds boy heard the weather-forecaster and asked his father: "Is that God talking?" "Why do you say that?" "Well - who else would know what the weather's going to do?"

A Craven postman emerged from his house to see a snowy landscape. He remarked: "I reckon what we need is a shower of paraffin - and a flash of lightning."

WEDDINGS

A nervous bridegroom said "I will" three times, twice in the wrong places. When, in the vestry, the vicar congratulated him and hoped he and his bride would have a happy married life, the bride-groom stammered and said: "Same to you, sir - and many of 'em."

At the wedding reception, the bride's father told the assembled guests that his daughter was fond of pets. "I hope," he added, "that the latest one is cleaner and eats less."

Tom was getting married for a second time. A friend attending the wedding observed to the next person in the pew: "You'd have thought he were owd enough to know better nor that." "Aye, he does know better, lad," was the reply, "but he met a widow who knew better still."

Beware of the lass who put on airs. "Winter sown wheat, and summer proud lass, won't fetch t'farmer varry much brass." And, in marriage, brass was not everything, for if you "wed t'midden for t'muck" you might get "puzzuned with t'stinks."

WOOLMEN

A wool merchant from Denholme was taken in hand by one of his apprentices who had been educated at a public school. He decided to teach the old, self-made man a lesson in politeness and courtesy by suggesting that when they were walking through the city centre he should raise his hat when greeting acquaintances. When surprise was expressed at the number of people the old man knew, he said: "Nay, lad - I'm nobbut practicing."

A Bradford woolman with idle sons said: "Look at me. Seventy years old and I still get up at four o' clock every morning, choose what time it is."

The Bradfordian displayed a sign outside his mill: "Second to None." On the following day, while passing the mill of a rival, he saw a sign: "None".

Two woolmen visited York Minster. One stared with such awe his friend remarked: "I'm glad you're impressed." His friend said: "I am, lad. Just imagine how many bales o' wool you could get in this place."

Heard at the old Bradford Wool Exchange: "Hes ta noticed how it's usually t'idle tongues 'at work overtime?"